NATURE'S MYSTERIES

GEYSERS
AND HOT SPRINGS

THERESE M. SHEA

Britannica
Educational Publishing

IN ASSOCIATION WITH

ROSEN
EDUCATIONAL SERVICES

Published in 2017 by Britannica Educational Publishing (a trademark of Encyclopædia Britannica, Inc.) in association with The Rosen Publishing Group, Inc.
29 East 21st Street, New York, NY 10010

Distributed exclusively by Rosen Publishing.
To see additional Britannica Educational Publishing titles, go to rosenpublishing.com.

First Edition

Britannica Educational Publishing
J.E. Luebering: Executive Director, Core Editorial
Mary Rose McCudden: Editor, Britannica Student Encyclopedia

Rosen Publishing
Shalini Saxena: Editor
Nelson Sá: Art Director
Michael Moy: Designer
Cindy Reiman: Photography Manager
Sherri Jackson: Photo Researcher

Library of Congress Cataloging-in-Publication Data

Names: Shea, Therese, author.
Title: Geysers and hot springs / Therese M. Shea.
Description: First edition. | New York : Britannica Educational Publishing in
  association with Rosen Educational Services, 2017. | 2017 | Series:
  Nature's mysteries | Includes bibliographical references and index.
Identifiers: LCCN 2015044297| ISBN 9781680484809 (library bound) | ISBN
  9781680484885 (pbk.) | ISBN 9781680484571 (6-pack)
Subjects: LCSH: Geysers—Juvenile literature. | Hydrothermal vents—Juvenile
  literature. | Hot springs—Juvenile literature.
Classification: LCC GB1198.5 S54 2017 | DDC 551.2/3—dc23
LC record available at http://lccn.loc.gov/2015044297

Manufactured in the United States of America

Photo credits: Cover, p. 1 Karen Bleier/AFP/Getty Images; cover, p. 1 (cloudburst graphic) Macrovector/Shutterstock.com; back cover, interior pages background image, p. 5 Tiago Lopes Fernandez/Shutterstock.com; p. 4 NASA/JPL; p. 6 Franco Origlia/Getty Images; p. 7 Anouk Noordhuizen/Shutterstock.com; p. 8 Encyclopædia Britannica, Inc.; p. 9 Richard Rasmussen/America 24-7/Getty Images; p. 10 Mike Blanchard/Shutterstock.com; p. 11 Ian Kennedy/Shutterstock.com; p. 12 bennymarty/iStock/Thinkstock; p. 13 Steve Gschmeissner/Science Source; p. 14 jesselindemann/iStock/Thinkstock; p. 15 Theodore Clutter/Science Source/ Getty Images; p. 16 photo by Dave Moore/Moment/Getty Images; p. 17 Alfredo Mancia/Moment/Getty Images; p. 18 Izzet Keribar/Lonely Planet Images/Getty Images; p. 19 Vadim Petrakov/Shutterstock.com; p. 20 Photo by William H. Jackson/U.S. National Park Service; p. 21 f11photo/Shutterstock.com; p. 22 gracious tiger/Shutterstock.com; p. 23 Carol Polich/Lonely Planet Images/Getty Images; p. 24 © Barbara Whitney; p. 25 ttsz/iStock/Thinkstock; p. 26 Inga Spence/Photolibrary /Getty Images; p. 27 © Niall Ferguson/Alamy Stock Photo; p. 28 © Prisma Bildagentur AG/Alamy Stock Photo; p. 29 © Buddy Mays/Alamy Stock Photo; interior pages background patterns Eky Studio/Shutterstock.com (rays), zffoto/Shutterstock.com (waves).

CONTENTS

WATER, WATER, EVERYWHERE

Liquid water is one of the essential elements for life on Earth.

Earth is sometimes called the "Blue Planet" because most of it is covered by water. Most of that water is salt water—about 97.5 percent. People and many other living things, however, need fresh water to live. Fresh water has little salt in it. Luckily, there are freshwater lakes, rivers, and glaciers. Another source, though, cannot be seen. About 30 percent

THINK ABOUT IT

People—and all life—need fresh water to live. In what ways do you use fresh water?

of Earth's fresh water is underground. Some of this comes out of the ground as natural springs.

Hot springs and geysers are two types of natural springs that reveal much about what goes on beneath Earth's surface. They tell us about the intense heat of inner Earth, about volcanic activity, and about other forces at work in nature. Hot springs and geysers are also popular places for people to visit.

Areas of the Atacama Desert of South America get no rainfall. However, underground water comes to the surface through geysers.

WHAT ARE SPRINGS?

The Vaucluse spring is the largest spring in France. Its waters are the source of the Sorgue River.

A spring is a place where water naturally flows from the ground. Springs develop when rainfall sinks through the soil to the rocks beneath. Some kinds of rock are porous, or full of little holes like sponges, and they absorb the water. Other rocks have cracks that allow the water to trickle through to lower layers of rock. Sometimes this underground water is under pressure and seeps upwards through an opening in level ground. A spring may come out of dry ground or into a stream, lake, or sea.

A hot spring, or **thermal** spring, is a spring with a water temperature much higher than the average air temperature of the surrounding area. Some hot springs emerge powerfully—with so much force that they eject tall columns of water and steam. These are called geysers.

The Mammoth Hot Springs are in Yellowstone National Park. Their flowing waters helped shape the land over thousands of years.

INSIDE EARTH

M ost hot springs occur near volcanoes or areas with volcanic activity. In these areas, the temperature inside Earth is very hot. The heat melts rock underground and forms a substance called magma. Hot magma underground heats up the groundwater. The water then tends to rise

This diagram shows how magma can heat groundwater that rises to Earth's surface, escaping through hot springs and geysers.

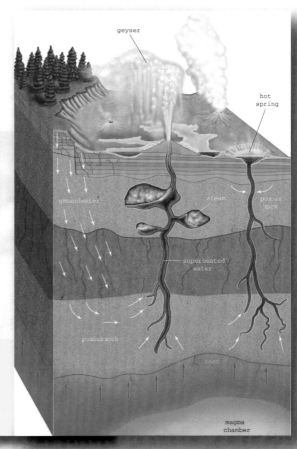

geyser

hot spring

groundwater

steam

porous rock

superheated water

porous rock

crust

magma chamber

Natural convection occurs when fluids are heated. When the fluid molecules are heated, the fluid becomes larger and lighter. The heated molecules take up more space and rise to the top while the cooler molecules sink to the bottom. These cooler molecules then become heated and the process is repeated.

toward the surface. It is channeled through a fault or some other fracture and forms a hot spring.

Some hot springs are not related to volcanic activity. The water is heated when groundwater moving downward reaches the lower parts of Earth's crust. The rocks there have high temperatures. **Natural convection** then occurs.

Water from this hot spring in Arkansas escapes into the cooler air as steam.

WHAT'S THAT SMELL?

Different elements and living organisms combine to color part of the Porcelain Basin of Yellowstone National Park.

Hot springs bring forth water that has picked up many substances along its underground journey. This matter may still be in the water that bubbles up from under the surface. Gases such as ammonia and methane may be present as well as elements such as iron and arsenic. There may be salts, too. These things can color the area around hot springs.

Some hot springs have an odor that smells much like rotten eggs. This reveals that there are substances called sulfides in the water. However, the sulfides do not cause the smell. Instead, the smell comes from a gas that is released when **bacteria** eat the sulfides.

Bacteria live in the hot water of Yellowstone National Park's Sulphur Caldron. The area is known for its very strong smell.

IT'S ALIVE!

Bacteria and other tiny living things such as algae also help make hot springs colorful. Many grow in huge colonies called mats. These form large colorful areas on the sides of hot springs. These microorganisms can give a hot spring several different colors, including yellow, orange, green, blue, and red.

Different colors in a hot spring are proof that different forms of life call it home.

THINK ABOUT IT

Scientists study living things that do well in hot places to learn about possible life on other planets. Why do you think this is?

Different kinds of organisms thrive in different surroundings. The temperature of a hot spring is one factor that determines what can live there. Some bacteria can grow at temperatures of up to 194° F (90° C). Algae in hot springs are most common at temperatures of 131° F (55° C) or below.

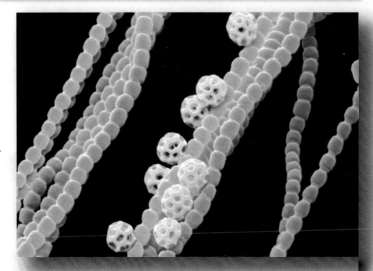

Cyanobacteria, in blue, can grow in conditions too harsh for other forms of life. Bacteria are much smaller than this in real life.

GUSHING GEYSERS

A geyser is a hot spring that sometimes erupts, sending steam and hot water gushing into the air. The steam comes from near-boiling water that is trapped in deep, narrow channels beneath the surface. In other hot springs, the hot water can move freely up to the surface, where it can cool down. In a geyser, the water does not have a direct route to the surface. It must move through a crooked tubelike opening that leads from the interior to the ground surface.

Strokkur is a geyser located in southwestern Iceland. It erupts every few minutes.

The heated water underground starts to turn to steam. As the steam rises, it pushes a little of the water above it out of the opening to the surface. There is then less water in the tube and therefore less pressure on the water deeper down. That water can boil and turn into more steam. The steam then expands and blows out with force, taking more hot water with it into the air. This chain reaction continues until the geyser exhausts its supply of boiling water.

This geyser is the result of a failed attempt to make a well. The water is much too hot to drink, though.

Geysers are sometimes classified by their vent, or the type of opening they have. A fountain-type geyser has a large opening that usually fills with water before or during an eruption. Steam and water sprays in all directions, somewhat like a fountain.

In many geysers, as water is ejected and cooled, a substance called dissolved silica collects on the ground at the surface. This matter is known as sinter. The sinter can pile into a mound that narrows the escape

Iceland's Strokkur is a fountain-type geyser. Notice the shape of its eruption.

THINK ABOUT IT

Pure silica is white. However, sometimes sinter deposits are different colors. Why do you think this is?

route of the steam and water. It acts like a nozzle when the eruption squirts out. This kind of geyser is called a cone geyser. Some cone geysers have been given fanciful names (such as Castle Geyser, in Yellowstone Park). These are based on the shapes formed by the sinter at the vents.

Castle Geyser is shown here. You can see the sinter mound through which the water erupts.

HUNTING FOR HOT SPRINGS AND GEYSERS

Iceland's geysers draw many visitors to the country.

Hot springs can be found on all continents, on land and in the oceans. However, geysers are much more rare. The term "geyser" comes from the Icelandic word *geysir*, meaning "to gush." The Great Geysir in southwestern Iceland gave its name to geysers around the world. Both hot springs and geysers form in areas with

COMPARE AND CONTRAST

Certain conditions are needed by hot springs and geysers. Why do you think one kind of spring is more common than the other?

volcanic activity. These areas usually lie along the boundaries between the large rocky plates that make up Earth's crust.

Sixteen geysers are found in Iceland, about forty geysers in New Zealand, two hundred on the Kamchatka Peninsula in the Russian Far East, and fifty scattered throughout the world in many other volcanic areas. There are more than three hundred geysers in Yellowstone National Park in the western United States—about half the world's total.

Russia's Valley of Geysers was discovered in 1941. Sadly, landslides have buried many of the geysers in recent years.

OLD FAITHFUL AND OTHER GEYSERS

Perhaps the most famous geyser is Old Faithful. It is located in northwestern Wyoming in Yellowstone National Park. It was given its name in 1870. The people who discovered the cone geyser said it spouted "faithfully" every 63 to 70 minutes. Today,

This is the oldest known photograph of Old Faithful erupting, taken in 1871.

THINK ABOUT IT

Old Faithful became less "faithful" after an earthquake in 1983. Why do you think this might this be?

most of Old Faithful's eruptions fall within a range of about 60 to 110 minutes, the average being about every 90 minutes.

The geyser's eruption can be predicted from one event to the next. The timing of each eruption is determined by the length of the eruption before it. So, the longer an eruption is, the longer the period to the next eruption. Old Faithful's eruptions last from 1.5 to 5.5 minutes.

Tourists watch Old Faithful, perhaps the most famous geyser in the world, erupt in Yellowstone National Park.

An eruption of Old Faithful can spout as much as 8,400 gallons (32,000 liters) of hot water. The water temperature at the geyser's opening is about 204°F (95.6 °C). The geyser shoots water an average of 135 feet (41 meters) in the air. The water can shoot higher than 180 feet (55 meters) at times.

However, Old Faithful is not even close to the tallest active geyser in the world. Steamboat Geyser, which is also located in Yellowstone, reaches heights of more

Steamboat Geyser's eruptions are an amazing sight. However, they can't be predicted.

THINK ABOUT IT

Geysers can be very dangerous. Why do you think this is?

than 300 feet (91 meters). It does not erupt very often.

The largest geyser ever recorded was Waimangu in New Zealand. It spouted water as well as mud and bits of rock. One eruption reached a height of over 1,510 feet (460 meters). The geyser erupted several times between 1900 and 1904, but it is no longer active.

The Grand Geyser of Yellowstone is the world's tallest geyser with predictable eruptions, reaching heights of 200 feet (61 meters).

SPRINGS OF ENERGY

The energy that heats the water inside Earth is called geothermal energy. People have learned how to use this energy for cooking, bathing, and heating. It can be converted into electricity as well. In some places, holes must be drilled down through rocks to reach the heat. In other places, the heat is so close to the surface that it can be used as an energy source easily. These are areas near active volcanoes or along plate boundaries—the same places where hot springs and geysers occur.

This geothermal power plant in Iceland provides energy to more than half of the nation's population.

PROTECTING GEYSERS AND HOT SPRINGS

This geothermal well in Nevada draws underground water to create geothermal energy.

Geysers draw their water from underground sources. These are basically natural lakes of hot water that are found under Earth's surface. In some places, such as near Yellowstone National Park, geothermal energy companies are setting up wells near geysers. They draw energy from the underground sources. Activity

COMPARE AND CONTRAST

Do you think it is better to preserve geysers or to allow geothermal energy development? Why?

like this has been known to "dry up" geysers. In New Zealand, more than 100 geysers have become extinct because of human activity.

Some people think there should be a "Geyser Protection Area" around Yellowstone, even beyond the boundaries of the park. They want to protect the underground sources of the geysers. They hope this will keep Old Faithful and other geysers and hot springs from becoming extinct.

This cone geyser has dried up. Some fear other geysers will do the same due to nearby geothermal energy use.

PRECIOUS NATURAL RESOURCES

Hot springs and geysers have long been places where people settle and tourists visit. In some areas, hot springs and cold springs mix to create pools of water where people can bathe comfortably. Some people believe the **minerals** present in such pools have special health benefits. Many towns in the United States and around the world are named for their thermal features,

Mineral waters shaped the Pamukkale Travertine Terraces of Turkey.

VOCABULARY

Minerals are nonliving substances that occur naturally. They make up Earth's rocks, sands, and soils.

including Hot Springs, Arkansas, and Warm Springs, Georgia.

People continue to flock to geysers in places like Yellowstone to see the spectacular show of steam and water spouting into the air. Both hot springs and geysers are impressive products of the power of Earth's processes. They are also a reminder of how precious and sometimes fragile our natural resources are.

The Tabacón Hot Springs of Costa Rica are warmed by magma—which also causes eruptions of a nearby volcano.

GLOSSARY

ALGAE Plantlike things that mostly live in water. Although they are like plants, they have no leaves, root, or stems.

AVERAGE A number obtained by adding a group of numbers together and then dividing the total by the amount of numbers.

CLASSIFIED Assigned to or arranged in groups.

COLONIES Groups of organisms of the same kind living together.

DISSOLVED Mixed with a liquid to become part of the liquid.

EJECT To cause something to burst out from something else with force.

EMERGE To arise, appear, or occur.

ERUPTS Ejects material from within.

EXHAUSTS Uses up all the resources contained within something.

EXTINCT No longer active or likely to erupt.

FAULT An opening in Earth's crust.

FRACTURE A break or split.

GLOBAL WARMING The slowly increasing average surface temperature on Earth. Many scientists believe global warming is caused by the increase of certain gases (such as carbon dioxide) in the atmosphere, or the layer of air that surrounds Earth.

MAGMA Hot, liquid rock inside Earth.

MICROORGANISM A tiny organism that can only be seen under a microscope.

MOLECULE A very small piece of matter, consisting of one or more atoms.

ORGANISM A living thing.

PREDICTED Declared in advance, based on current events or past experiences.

VENT An opening through which gas or liquid escapes in order to relieve pressure.

VOLCANO An opening in a planet's surface through which hot, liquid rock sometimes flows.

FOR MORE INFORMATION

Books

Frisch, Nate. *Yellowstone National Park*. Mankato, MN: Creative Education, 2014.

Jennings, Terry J. *Violent Volcanoes*. Mankato, MN: Smart Apple Media, 2010.

Magloff, Lisa. *Experiments with Heat and Energy*. New York, NY: Gareth Stevens Publishing, 2010.

Owen, Ruth. *Energy from Inside Our Planet: Geothermal Power*. New York, NY: PowerKids Press, 2013.

Wachtel, Alan, and Debra Voege. *Geothermal Energy*. New York, NY: Chelsea Clubhouse, 2010.

Websites

Because of the changing nature of Internet links, Rosen Publishing has developed an online list of websites related to the subject of this book. This site is updated regularly. Please use this link to access this list:

http://www.rosenlinks.com/NMY/geyser

INDEX

COMPARE AND CONTRAST

Fossil fuels can take thousands or millions of years to form. Why are they considered nonrenewable resources while geothermal energy is renewable?

Geothermal energy is a renewable resource—or a natural resource that cannot be used up. Other resources, such as oil, coal, and natural gas, are considered nonrenewable. They are called fossil fuels because they come from fossils. Fossils are the remains of plants and animals from long ago. Many people think that fossil fuels also contribute to a problem called global warming. Geothermal energy is considered a cleaner source of energy.

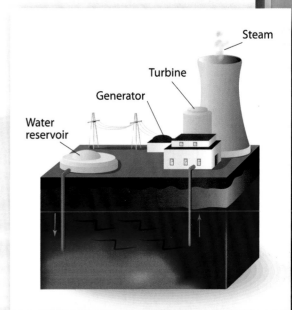

Geothermal power plants use Earth's hot water and steam as energy sources.